Moashella Shortte is the proud mother of four beautiful children. As a mom and educator, she has been creating and sharing children stories for many years. Growing up on a tiny Caribbean island where books were at a premium, she treasured each that came her way, and when there was none, she made up stories with inspiration coming from her beautiful home and the colorful characters that were her fellow islanders. The only thing that can top her passion for books and storytelling is her love for children, so there is little wonder that she wants the first story she shares with the world to be a children's book.

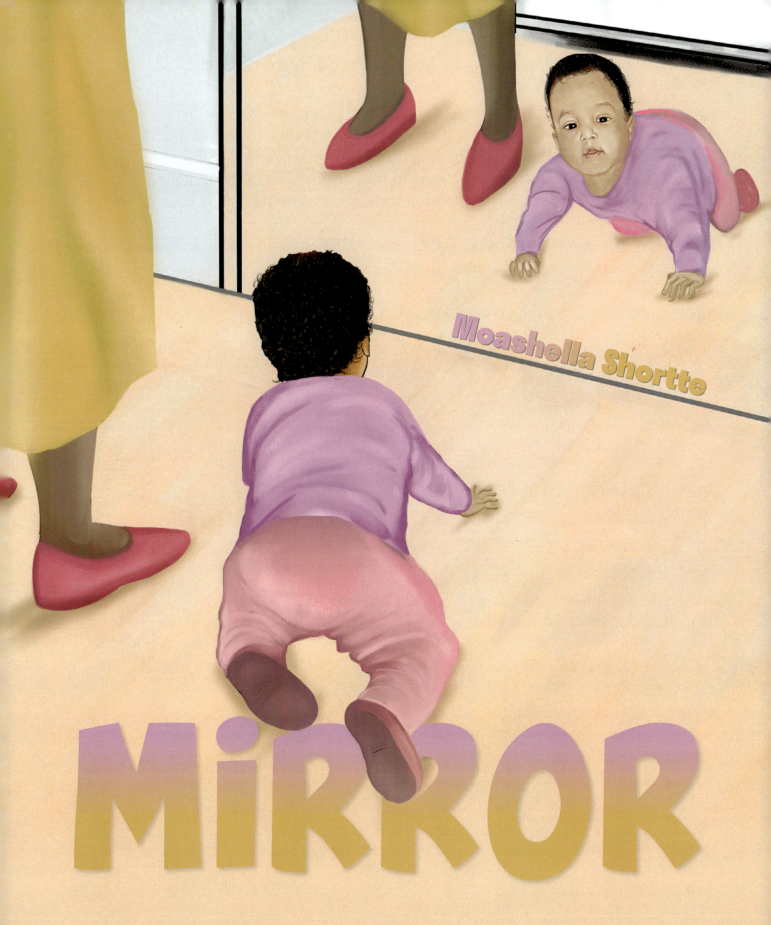

Moashella Shortte

MIRROR

AUSTIN MACAULEY PUBLISHERS
LONDON • CAMBRIDGE • NEW YORK • SHARJAH

Copyright © Moashella Shortte (2020)

All rights reserved. No part of this publication may be reproduced, distributed, or transmitted in any form or by any means, including photocopying, recording, or other electronic or mechanical methods, without the prior written permission of the publisher, except in the case of brief quotations embodied in critical reviews and certain other noncommercial uses permitted by copyright law. For permission requests, write to the publisher.

Any person who commits any unauthorized act in relation to this publication may be liable to criminal prosecution and civil claims for damages.

Austin Macauley is committed to publishing works of quality and integrity. In that spirit, we are proud to offer this book to our readers; however, the story, the experiences, and the words are the author's alone.

Ordering Information:
Quantity sales: special discounts are available on quantity purchases by corporations, associations, and others. For details, contact the publisher at the address below.

Publisher's Cataloging-in-Publication data
Shortte, Moashella
Mirror

ISBN 9781643788753 (Paperback)
ISBN 9781643788746 (Hardback)
ISBN 9781645365464 (ePub e-book)

Library of Congress Control Number: 2020902979

www.austinmacauley.com/us

First Published (2020)
Austin Macauley Publishers LLC
40 Wall Street, 28th Floor
New York, NY 10005
USA

mail-usa@austinmacauley.com
+1 (646) 5125767

For My Children:
Micah, my joy
Mateo, my sunshine
Siena, my angel
Sacha, my heart-born son

Heartfelt gratitude to Dany and Nat, for their unwavering support and encouragement.

For my sweet Siena

***

You are a dream come true
And so much more.
My wish for you is that you will know
your value and that you will
treat yourself with the
sweetest of kindness,
always!
Love you beyond eternity,
Mom

I look in the mirror and who do I see?
It's her! She's back, like I thought she would be.

I love her and will always tell her so.
I will give her all she needs to develop and grow.

To her I will always be kind, gentle and sweet.
And give big smiles whenever we meet.

I will tell her the truth and never lie.
I will be there for her if ever she cries.

I will come to see her everyday
And stay for a while if she wants it that way.

She's special, she's wonderful,
and she's one of a kind.

And with her I will be forever and a while.

So I look in the mirror and who do I see?
I see exactly the person that I want to be

I see me!